D1220838

Metric Can Be Fun!

Written and Illustrated by Munro Leaf

J. B. Lippincott Company   Philadelphia and New York

U.S. Library of Congress Cataloging in Publication Data

Leaf, Munro, birth date
  Metric can be fun!

  SUMMARY: Explains the terms of the metric system and suggests a few
exercises for practicing using these measurements.
  1. Metric system—Juvenile literature. [1. Metric system] I. Title.
QC92.5.L4   389'.152   75-29223
ISBN-0-397-31679-8   ISBN-0-397-31680-1 (pbk.)

For thousands of years people have been trying to measure things. We need a way to tell other people how far away a place is or how long or wide an object is. We need a way to describe how heavy something is or how much liquid is in a bottle.

If you told a friend that you had some gumdrops at home that you'd like to sell him, how would your friend know he was interested if you didn't have a way to measure how many gumdrops you had to sell and how far he'd have to travel to get them?

People in different places developed their own ways of measuring, and almost none of them was like anybody else's. When all these different countries began to do a lot of trading with one another, people had almost as many problems understanding what was being talked about as they would have had if they had had no system of measurement at all.

If people all over the world were going to be talking with one another about the measurement of things, we needed one system that everybody could use. Scientists in France developed the metric system and, in 1799, it was adopted for use everywhere in France. Today most countries in the world use the metric system.

The United States and England are nearly the last to change from their old systems, but both will make the change soon. When everybody measures things the same way, exchanging information and goods around the world will be simpler.

In this book we are going to follow the advice of Dr. Alexander Graham Bell (the man who invented the telephone). Dr. Bell used metric measurement when he worked on inventions because he found it made it easier for him to solve problems.

He thought it would be better for the people who worked with him to use metric too.

When he opened a new laboratory in Nova Scotia, he decided to teach the system to all his employees. It worked so well that Dr. Bell tried to talk the United States Congress into adopting the system for the whole country.

But most of the congressmen thought the metric system would be too hard. Dr. Bell tried to change their minds. He told them, "All the difficulties in the metric system are in translating from one system to the other, but the moment you use the metric system alone there is no difficulty."

That was in 1906. If Congress had listened to Dr. Bell and the others who agreed with him, today our old way of measuring would be a thing of the past.

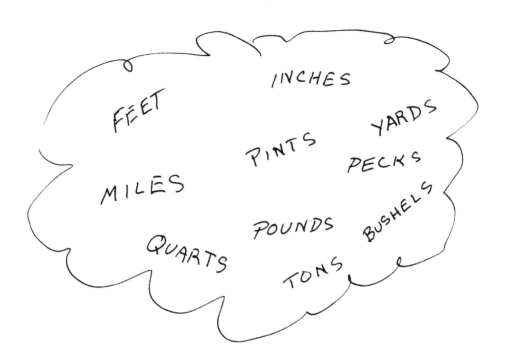

Now we will begin. Forget that you have ever heard of inches, feet, yards, miles; or pints, quarts, pounds, tons and pecks and bushels. You don't need the old way to learn the new way. When you get used to it, you will see that the metric system is both quick and easy. It can even be fun!

In the metric system each unit of measurement has its own name. Each unit is *ten times* more than the next smaller unit.

MORE THAN 1 METER
A **DECA**METER is 10 meters
A **HECTO**METER is 100 meters
A **KILO**METER is 1000 meters

LESS THAN 1 METER
A **DECI**METER is $\frac{1}{10}$ of a meter. Another way to say it is that it takes 10 decimeters to make a meter.

A **CENTI**METER is $\frac{1}{100}$ of a meter. Another way to say it is that it takes 100 centimeters to make a meter.

A **MILLI**METER is $\frac{1}{1000}$ of a meter. Another way to say it is that it takes 1000 millimeters to make a meter.

The METER is used to measure length. To find out how long one meter is we will make a meter stick.

You will need a straight stick or a piece of cardboard ten times longer than this line.

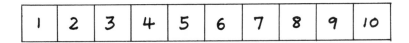

The distance between one mark and the next on the line above is a CEN-TIMETER long. Ten centimeters are called a DECIMETER. Ten decimeters (one hundred centimeters) are called a METER.

Mark your stick to show ten decimeters or one hundred centimeters and you will have a ruler one meter long.

This line is one centimeter long. When you divide a centimeter into ten equal parts, each mark is one MILLIMETER from the next. We don't need to measure millimeters very often, but there are one thousand of them in a meter.

Once we know how long a meter is, we can measure the length, width, and height of anything.

When we speak of long distances, such as how far New York is from California, we measure them in KILOMETERS. Pretty soon signs on the road will tell you how many kilometers it is from one place to another instead of how many miles.

You can use your meter stick with decimeters and centimeters marked on it to find out how tall people are. You can measure how high your window is off the floor, how tall your desk is, or how long and how wide your room is.

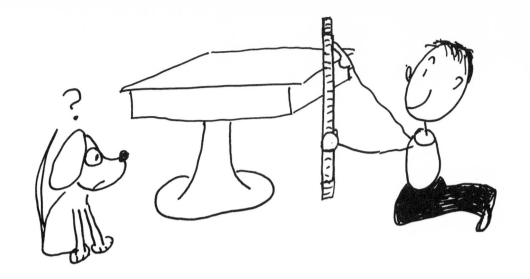

The girl in this picture has measured a rug and found out that it is 3 meters long and 2 meters wide. Now she wants to know what the PERIMETER of the rug is. Two sides measure 3 meters each and two sides measure 2 meters each. So we say its PERIMETER, which means the distance around the edges of anything, is

$$
\begin{array}{r}
3 \text{ meters} \\
+ \\
3 \text{ meters} \\
+ \\
2 \text{ meters} \\
+ \\
\underline{2 \text{ meters}} \\
10 \text{ meters}
\end{array}
$$

Find out what the perimeter of your bed is. That is how far it is all the way around the four sides.

What is the perimeter of your house? What is the perimeter of your dog's house?

If you don't have a dog—measure your cat's box.

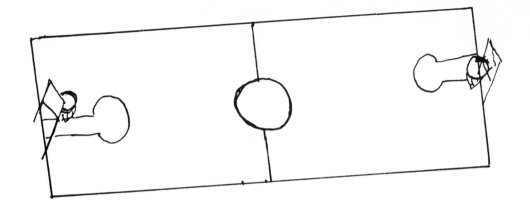

Or if you don't have either, find out what the perimeter of a basketball court is or how far it is from home plate on a baseball field to first base to second to third and home again. The combined measurement of the outside edges of any object is its perimeter.

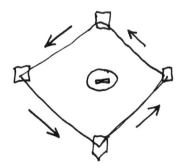

Now that we know what the perimeter of a surface is, let's learn how we can measure the whole surface—not just the outside edges.

The rug the girl measured was 3 meters long and 2 meters wide and had a perimeter of 10 meters, but there is more to a rug than its outside edges. The entire surface of any object is its AREA.

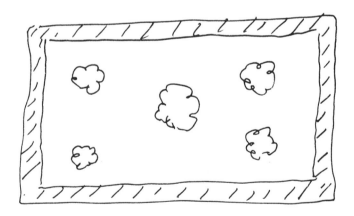

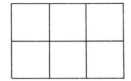

This drawing is 3 centimeters long and 2 centimeters wide. To find out the area the drawing covers, we multiply the length by the width. 3 centimeters times 2 centimeters equals 6 square centimeters. In other words, the surface area this drawing covers is six square centimeters.

Surfaces can be measured in square centimeters or square decimeters or square meters or square kilometers. To find out how many square centimeters, decimeters, meters, or kilometers there are in a surface, you always multiply the length by the width. The answer you get is called the AREA of the surface.

How many square centimeters are in this area?

How many in this one?

Measure the top of a table or your bed or a book. What are the areas of their surfaces?

We now know how to measure length, width, height, and distance. We can also measure perimeter and area. What else do we need to know how to measure?

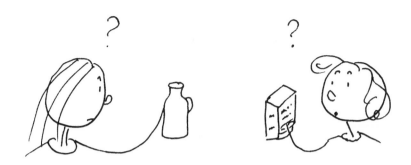

We still don't know how to measure the QUANTITY of things such as flour, rice, apples, coffee, sugar, meat, or potatoes. We also don't know how to measure liquids such as milk, water, gasoline, or oil. Let's find out how QUANTITY is measured in metric.

Finding out how much of anything is in a can, a bottle, or a box is not hard to do because the metric system uses measurements that are like those we've already learned about.

You know that a square meter would look like this:

1 meter long

$\times$

1 meter wide

1 square meter

Now, suppose you have a box with sides that measure 1 square meter each. An object with six equal square sides is called a CUBE. The dice you roll when you play Parcheesi or backgammon or other games are little cubes.

To find out how much your cube-shaped box can hold, you multiply the height times the width times the length.

$$1 \text{ meter}$$
$$\times$$
$$1 \text{ meter}$$
$$\times$$
$$\underline{1 \text{ meter}}$$
$$1 \text{ cubic meter}$$

Another name for the cubic meter is the STERE, but you won't use this name very much.

A CUBIC METER is much too big to be a useful unit of measurement for most of the liquids you will want to know about. If you poured a glass of milk into a box that would hold a cubic meter, it would barely cover the bottom.

1 CUBIC METER

The LITER is our common unit of measurement for liquids. There are one thousand liters in a cubic meter. In other words, a cubic meter is one thousand times bigger than a liter. You can see that it makes sense to use the liter to measure most liquids.

This is how big a LITER box would be.

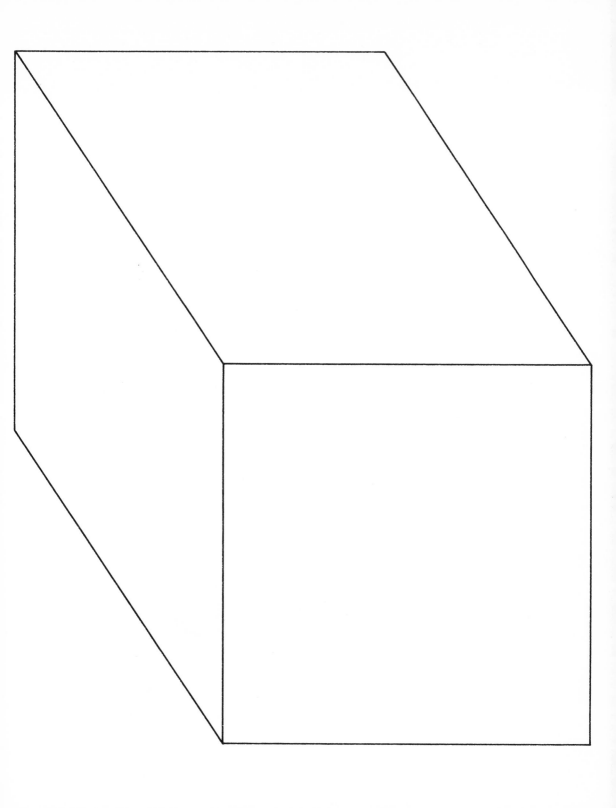

Each side measures 10 centimeters.

$$
\begin{array}{c}
\text{10 centimeters} \\
\times \\
\text{10 centimeters} \\
\times \\
\underline{\text{10 centimeters}} \\
\text{1000 cubic centimeters}
\end{array}
$$

A box that measures 1000 cubic centimeters will hold one LITER.

In the metric system the LITER is the unit we most often use to measure liquids.

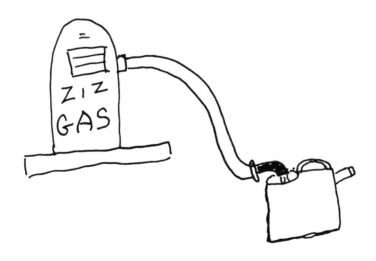

We use the same prefixes that we learned with the meter to show that each unit is *ten times* more than the next smaller unit.

MORE THAN 1 LITER
    A **DECA**LITER is 10 liters
    A **HECTO**LITER is 100 liters
    A **KILO**LITER is 1000 liters

LESS THAN 1 LITER
A **DECI**LITER is $\frac{1}{10}$ of a liter. Another way to say it is that it takes 10 deciliters to make a liter.

A **CENTI**LITER is $\frac{1}{100}$ of a liter. Another way to say it is that it takes 100 centiliters to make a liter.

A **MILLI**LITER is $\frac{1}{1000}$ of a liter. Another way to say it is that it takes 1000 milliliters to make a liter.

You can make a box that will have enough room inside to hold a liter of liquid. On a piece of paper, draw a square that measures 10 centimeters on each side. Cut out six of these squares and tape them together to form a cube. You won't be able to measure liquids with your liter cube, but making one will give you an idea of how big a liter is.

Your school may have a liter measure with marks on it to show how many centiliters are in it. Many stores now have liter measures for sale. The next time you visit your doctor, ask him to show you the syringe he gives injections with. You will see that the tube is marked to tell how much of a liter it holds.

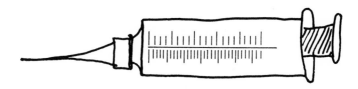

This small box measures ONE CUBIC CENTIMETER. The liter cube you just made can hold one thousand cubic centimeters. When we want to measure only a small amount of liquid, we measure in cubic centimeters.

Now comes an interesting thing about the metric system:

If you filled the liter box with pure water that is not too hot or too cold, the water would weigh just about ONE KILOGRAM. The GRAM is the unit of measurement commonly used for weight in the metric system. Since a kilogram is a thousand grams and a liter is a thousand cubic centimeters, we know that one gram of water is equal to one cubic centimeter of water. We call this amount of liquid a MILLILITER.

And now we have come to HOW MUCH DOES IT WEIGH? Weight in the metric system is usually expressed in GRAMS. We use the same prefixes that we learned with the meter and the liter to show that each unit is *ten times* more than the next smaller unit.

MORE THAN 1 GRAM

    A **DECA**GRAM is 10 grams

    A **HECTO**GRAM is 100 grams

    A **KILO**GRAM is 1000 grams

LESS THAN 1 GRAM

    A **DECI**GRAM is $\frac{1}{10}$ of a gram. Another way to say it is that it takes 10 decigrams to make a gram.

    A **CENTI**GRAM is $\frac{1}{100}$ of a gram. Another way to say it is that it takes 100 centigrams to make a gram.

    A **MILLI**GRAM is $\frac{1}{1000}$ of a gram. Another way to say it is that it takes 1000 milligrams to make a gram.

The only way for you to measure for yourself the metric weight of an object is to use a scale that gives weight in grams. However, if you don't have a metric scale, you can get an idea of how much the units represent by looking at the labels of some products that are available in stores by metric weight.

LOOK IN DRUGSTORES

AND SUPERMARKETS

AT CANS BOTTLES BOXES

AND LOOK AT THE PRINTING ON THEM

Vitamin tablets are labeled according to how much of a particular vitamin they contain. Vitamin C, for instance, can be bought in 100, 250, or 500 milligram amounts. By looking at the different sizes of the tablets, you can get a general idea of how small those units of weight are.

If you have a baby brother or sister, he or she probably weighed from 2 to 4 kilograms at birth. Your father may weigh about 80 kilograms; your mother may weigh about 60 kilograms. A baby elephant can weigh as much as 100 kilograms at birth and grow up to weigh more than *two* metric tons! The METRIC TON is one million (1,000,000) grams.

SUPERMARKET

PRODUCE

HE DOESN'T CARE HOW
THEY WEIGH IT.

JUST LET HIM AT IT.

Most of the things we buy by weight at the grocery store will be sold to us in kilograms. Twelve apples will probably weigh about two kilograms. Most people buy about two and one-half kilograms of flour or sugar at a time.

HOW HOT OR COLD IS IT?

We measure heat by degrees on a thermometer. There are three kinds of thermometers in use today: Kelvin (used by scientists), Fahrenheit (the one people in the United States use most often now), and the Celsius or centigrade thermometer, which is used in most of the countries already on the metric system.

When we change over to the metric system it makes sense to also change to the Celsius (centigrade) thermometer. A man named Anders Celsius, who lived more than two hundred years ago, thought of marking a thermometer in centigrades. He marked the freezing point of water at 0 degrees and the boiling point at 100 degrees.

FAHRENHEIT

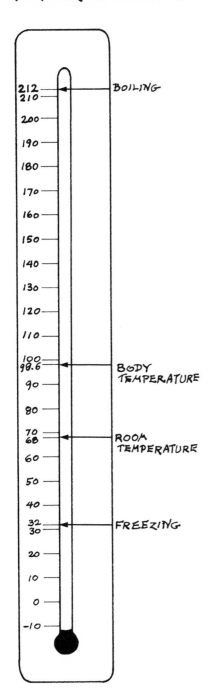

212 — ← BOILING
210 —
200 —
190 —
180 —
170 —
160 —
150 —
140 —
130 —
120 —
110 —
100 —
98.6 — ← BODY TEMPERATURE
90 —
80 —
70 —
68 — ← ROOM TEMPERATURE
60 —
50 —
40 —
32 — ← FREEZING
30 —
20 —
10 —
0 —
-10 —

CELSIUS

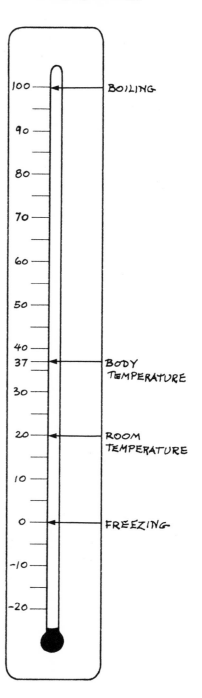

100 — ← BOILING
90 —
80 —
70 —
60 —
50 —
40 —
37 — ← BODY TEMPERATURE
30 —
20 — ← ROOM TEMPERATURE
10 —
0 — ← FREEZING
-10 —
-20 —

If you listen to TV or radio weather reports, you will notice that more and more of them already give the temperature in Celsius (centigrade) degrees, as well as in Fahrenheit degrees. On a

January evening you may hear that it is minus 45 degrees centigrade (−45°C) in Alaska, 2 degrees centigrade (2°C) in Princeton, New Jersey, and 50 degrees centigrade (50°C) in San Diego.

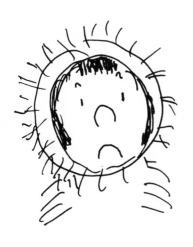

As we move closer and closer to the day when we will be using the metric system in the United States, we will see more things around us that make understanding the metric system important.

We know how long a meter is, and once we know that, if somebody tells us that Chicago is so many kilometers away, we understand that it is so many thousands of meters from where we are.

We can find out that it is so many centimeters or parts of a meter from one side
of the page in this book to the other.
Or that your mother or father is so many
meters or parts of a meter tall.

We can measure and add all the sides of anything flat to find out what its perimeter is. Then if we want to know how many square meters or parts of a meter are in the whole surface of an area, we can find that out too.

When we come to measuring a box or cube, we see how the metric system fits together. The capacity or volume of a cube shows what quantity or how much of anything solid or liquid it can hold. A liter box or cube we use for measuring liquids is ten centimeters by ten centimeters by ten centimeters (one thousand cubic centimeters). When it is filled with water, the water weighs one kilogram.

The water held by just one cubic centimeter is only one milliliter, and it weighs one gram. Kilograms and grams are our most used measures of weight.

REMEMBER THE CUBIC
CENTIMETER OF WATER
WEIGHS
1 GRAM

AND THE
LITER
OF
WATER
THAT IS A THOUSAND
CUBIC CENTIMETERS
WEIGHS
1 KILOGRAM

Look around you when you go to a supermarket and see how many cans and boxes have marked on them how many kilograms or grams are inside, or how many bottles and jugs have liters or parts of liters marked on them. When you go to a drugstore, see how many bottles or boxes of pills or medicines are marked in milliliters or milligrams.

YOU WILL SEE
A LOT

See how many road signs give distances
in kilometers.

You will discover that we've already begun to make some of the changes we must in order to join other countries of the world in using the same system of measuring things.

If you have a head start on learning about the system—then Metric Can Be Fun!

When you've used the metric system for a while, or if you've never used any other system, you won't need to refer to the old way of measuring things. But if you want to know the equivalent U.S. measuring units to the metric units used in this book, here they are:

LINEAR MEASURE

One inch is 25.4 millimeters, 2.54 centimeters, .0254 meter.
One foot is 30.48 centimeters, .3048 meter.
One yard is 91.44 centimeters, .9144 meter.
One mile is 1609.3472 meters, 1.609347 kilometers.

———————————

One millimeter is .03937 inch.
One meter is 3.28083 feet, 1.093611 yards.
One kilometer is .62137 mile.

SQUARE MEASURE

One square inch is 6.452 square centimeters.
One square foot is .0929 square meter.
One square yard is .8361 square meter.
One acre is .4047 hectare.
One square mile is 2.59 square kilometers.

One square centimeter is .155 square inch.
One square meter is 10.764 square feet, 1.196 square yards.
One hectare is 2.471 acres.
One square kilometer is .3861 square mile.

CUBIC MEASURE

One cubic inch is 16.3872 cubic centimeters.
One cubic foot is .028317 cubic meter.
One cubic yard is .7646 cubic meter.

One cubic centimeter is .06102 cubic inch.
One cubic meter is 35.314 cubic feet, 1.3079 cubic yards.

QUANTITY, DRY MEASURE

One pint is .550 liters.
One quart is 1.101 liters.
One peck is 8.809 liters.
One bushel is 35.238 liters.

One deciliter is .18 pint.
One liter is .908 quart.
One decaliter is 1.14 pecks.
One hectoliter is 2.84 bushels.

One pint is .473 liter.
One quart is .946 liter.
One gallon is 3.785 liters.

One deciliter is .21 pint.
One liter is 1.057 quarts.
One decaliter is 2.64 gallons.

WEIGHT
(avoirdupois)

One ounce is 28.349 grams.
One pound is .45359 kilogram.
One ton (2000 pounds) is .907 metric ton.

One gram is .035 ounce.
One decagram is .353 ounce.
One hectogram is 3.527 ounces.
One kilogram is 2.2046 pounds.
One metric ton is 1.1 tons.

About the Author

For many years Munro Leaf has been delighting and instructing young readers with his amusing stories and lively drawings. He is well known for his *Can Be Fun* books and has been a popular lecturer for children all over the world. Mr. Leaf now lives with his wife in Washington, D.C., where he devotes much of his time to developing educational aids for underprivileged children.